# SASQUATCH SENIOR COMMUNITY

---

## SASQUATCH SENIOR COMMUNITY
### BOOK 1

## PATRICK TALMADGE

HANGAR 1 PUBLISHING

# 1

## 1980 ORMOND BEACH FLORIDA IRON HORSE SALOON

It was a warm summer night in 1980, and the Iron Horse Saloon was having their first live band on their open-air stage In Ormond Beach Florida. The Iron Horse Saloon had been built next to the railroad tracks in an area with no houses, so they could blast the live music with no complaints. On the other side of the tracks was a creek and hidden behind the trees was a clear spring-fed pool that the local animals had used for thousands of years. When the first note sounded, every forest animal within a mile was startled and ran away except for one. That one animal was not afraid of the music, instead, it was drawn to the deep bass beat of the drums and the high notes of the guitars, and it especially loved the range of keyboards. This animal knew its troupe would love to hear this sound. It did not know what was making those sounds, but liked the sound and was going to investigate.

So as the other forest animals ran in fear of this, one called for others of its troupe to join it. When three more of its kind came to the call, it signaled for them to be quiet and follow. The four used the forest cover as they crept closer to the source of the noise.

These animals used the railroad tracks to travel unseen throughout their range. The railroad tracks were much easier when they wanted to move quickly and were not worried about being seen. They have learned to stay out of sight of the hairless one that lives in boxes in the area. A group of four males left the safety of the pool and crossed over the railroad tracks toward where that loud noise was coming from. They knew that the hairless ones had built one of their boxes over there, but the boxes that the hairless ones lived in had never made loud noises like this one is, before. As the four climbed the bank on the other side of the tracks, the hairless one's light became visible.

Somehow the hairless ones were able to make light anywhere they wanted to, and they could even carry it in their hands. Lights like the ones the hairless ones carry would be good for seeing in the bigger caves they used for living in, thought the leader. There were plenty of shadows to hide in even though the hairless ones had cleared most of the trees to build their box. What was unusual about this box was that it had a large flat box, which the hairless ones were standing on, and making the strange noises they had heard from the forest. Some of the hairless ones on the flat spot were holding things they moved that made that wonderful noise. There was one hairless one sitting down hitting round things that made the sound of a stick hitting a hollow log. The noise was too loud this close, but from the pool the noise was enjoyable.

The four crept back across the tracks to their pool, to enjoy the sounds in safety. The one who had heard the noise first was the leader of this troupe and wanted the rest of the troupe to come hear this wonderful sound. He signaled the others to run quickly to gather the troupe to the pond to listen to the sounds. As the others ran to gather his troupe, he sat on a log and listened. Without warning this animal stood at its full height, and let out a deep, loud, long, call. This was no normal call you'd hear in the woods. This call could be heard for miles through the thick Florida trees and vines. The call was so loud, the hairless ones at the box, across the railroad tracks making the noise, heard it, over the noise they were making, stopped moving, and became silent.

The animal making that incredible noise is not your regular Florida forest or swamp dweller. This usually quiet and reclusive animal is a 10-foot tall 1200-pound gigantic ape. As far as modern science this giant ape had died out millions of years ago. The indigenous peoples of the world know they still roam the earth. For the last couple hundred years since humans began hunting them with those loud noise sticks that throw small killing rocks, they have stayed hidden. He knew he was taking a chance, bringing his troupe to listen, but felt the pool gave enough cover, especially in the dark, and the noise the hairless ones were making was worth the chance. He was the leader of the troupe and if he thought it was safe it was good enough because he was 'Gu,' and 'Gu' is the leader of all the troupes in this forest.

The hairless ones began making their noise after a minute of pause. They had been making their talking sounds to one another after he made his call. He had gotten excited listening to the noise the hairless ones were making, lost control, and called out in happiness. He would have to use better control, and let the troupe know to use self-control when listening, so the hairless ones do not look for them. Gu listened to the wonderful noise as members of the troupe one by one gathered around the pool to listen in fascination to the strange sound the hairless ones were making. As each member arrived Gu signaled them to be absolutely silent, or they would have to leave. Not a single troupe member made a sound as they swayed and listened to the wonderful noise. Gu delighted in seeing his troupe so happy and thought he would have a troupe member stay near the pool at all times to alert the rest if the hairless ones make this music again.

It didn't take long for Gu to figure out which days the hairless ones met at that box to make that interesting noise. This was not like a normal hairless one's box that they live in all the time. The hairless ones only came here at night for two days, then for 5 days they were there in the daytime, but no noise outside. To make sure the troupe was extra safe from the hairless ones Gu instructed his troupe to build a thick brush wall between the pool and the railroad tracks that the hairless ones would not be able to see or walk through. The hairless ones are very weak and unable to walk through thick bushes or swamps. They build hard wide trails and sit in their shiny boxes that move them around, so they never go into the deep brush, which means the troupe will be safe. When they had finished, the pool was surrounded by a thick wall. They had many flat moss-covered areas for sleeping, sitting, and listening.

Gu and his troupe enjoyed a few uninterrupted seasons of the wonderful noise. They built a fantastic listening spot. The thick wall they had built between their pool and the tracks was absolutely impenetrable by the hairless ones but did not lessen the sounds the hairless ones made. The main entry to their safe listening grotto, was on the opposite side of the pool from the railroad tracks, so they could enter without needing to be on the tracks. Everything was wonderful until the day the hairless ones began clearing their forest near the pool.

In the year 1982, the Trails Company decided with all the seniors moving to Florida, they should cash in on the boom, and began building Bear Creek, a senior community. The only problem is that it was in Gu's troupe's territory. After many days the hairless ones cleared the forest right up to the edge of their pool. It was bad enough to have the hairless ones take their land, but they cleared right up to their pool, which meant they had to make a new entrance. Once Gu was pleased with their new entrance, he closed up the original one to keep them safe from the new hairless ones building the box next to the first entrance. It was a full season before the hairless ones finished building their boxes, and the first of them moved into the box by their pool. Gu would keep a close eye on the hairless ones, but his troupe was going to continue to listen to the wonderful noise twice a week at their pool.

## 2

# 1984 LOIS MOVES IN

984 was a horrible year for Lois. Her Husband died of cancer, and she was left alone after 25 years of marriage. Her two daughters were full grown, and each lived out of state with their own families. She and her husband had a business they ran together, which she decided to sell now that he was gone. After selling her home, and the business, Lois had enough money to retire, in real comfort. The family around her was loving, but her personal life was too much for her, so she planned to move. Lois didn't tell a soul about her plans. While she was selling everything she didn't need, she began looking for a new home. After living in Washington state for most of her life she wanted warmth for a change.

Earlier in the day she had picked up one of those newspaper-sized real estate sales magazines, which had homes throughout the United States, and began looking. There was an advertisement for a new senior community in Ormond Beach, Florida which looked promising. It was just being built, so everything was brand new. It was her perfect opportunity to start over, and the name was promising. Bear Creek was the name of the senior community. Lois's late husband loved bears, so she took this as a sign and gave them a call. After half a dozen calls to them talking about the property, a few letters including a map of how the community was laid out, and Lois was sold. She booked a flight to Daytona Beach, Florida to see the property. Lois was at SeaTac airport when she got called to the ticket counter to pick up a phone call. The news from the call was that her house was sold minutes before. Lois took this as another sign she was to move to Bear Creek.

When Lois got to Bear Creek, she was very impressed with all the amenities, and that the whole community was completely surrounded by thick trees, and brush and was basically a jungle. She had lived and raised her family on a small lake in rural Washington state that was surrounded by trees and cow pastures. When they showed her the last house on a dead-end road, she instantly fell in love with it. Lois took a long slow walk around the yard. The real estate agent went into the home and let Lois take all the time she needed. The agent recognized Lois wanted it but was in deep thought. After almost 30 minutes, Lois came into the home, looked at the agent, and said she would take it. The agent asked her if she wanted to look inside before she decided, and Lois said she would be spending all her time outside, so the inside wasn't a concern, and she was sure it would work out. Lois asked the agent to please fetch the paperwork, while she looked around outside a bit more, and they could sign the papers at the house.

When the agent returned to the home, Lois was sitting on the front step gazing off into the distance. It took the agent a couple of tries to get Lois's attention; she was so deep in thought. Lois gave a little start when she came back to reality, smiled at the agent, and asked for a pen, so she could sign before anyone else had a chance to steal it from her, because this felt like home to her. Once the papers were signed Lois went to her hotel in Daytona Beach and got dinner. After dinner, she took a walk on the beach. It was summer and hot to most people, but Lois had always loved the heat, and with the beach wind it was wonderful. Lois knew she was going to love Florida and her little piece of hidden heaven at Bear Creek. After two days of sightseeing, Lois headed back to Washington state to pack, and ship the rest of her worldly possessions to her new home, then move 3200 miles.

Lois returned home, sold the remaining things she didn't want, shipped her final boxes, and flew to Florida for a new beginning. Lois told her few close friends she was leaving before she left, then waited until she was in her new home before she let the rest of her friends and relatives know what she did. Lois didn't want to listen to arguments about why she shouldn't move and live alone in a new place. She wondered what they would think if she told them her home was at the end of a dead end in the middle of a jungle. Her final trump card to get them to shut up was to let them know it was a gated community with a guard.

There wasn't another home near Lois's home, because of a small creek that splits her property from the rest of the community. The construction company decided to build this single home at the end of the road, knowing someone would prefer privacy. Lois needed privacy because she played the piano and wanted an outdoor music cottage. This home was at least 500 feet from the nearest home. The best part was there was plenty of thick, brush and trees to stop the sound. Typical of a jungle, the vines around her house wove a thick blanket in the trees, that stopped most sounds.

Lois arrived at the new house about 30 minutes before the moving truck arrived. She had just enough time to map out where she was going to put things before the van pulled up. She honestly had no idea what the home looked like inside. She was so enchanted with the property and its seclusion, that she ignored the inside of the house and its layout. Luckily, she had sold most of her furniture, because she wanted to decorate it light, and airy maybe even with white wicker furniture, she mused. The movers took less than 2 hours to unload, and another 3 hours to place the furniture in its proper place, which took a substantial tip from Lois to get them to agree to do it.

# 3

## LOIS FINDS THE POOL

Two weeks after she moved, Lois was finally settled in enough to relax and take the time to really explore her gardens. The builders had left many of the natural larger trees and bushes that were on the perimeter and throughout the yard to add shade for the home. Once the builders cleared the land, they designed natural-looking gardens around her house to complement the natural surroundings. They had planted palm trees, amongst the old oak trees, and there were plants and bushes with colors Lois could have only dreamed of in Washington. The front and side yards were fully sculptured as one would expect for a gated community, even though she had no neighbors to see it. The back yard had a nice deck with steps down to the grass. Then 50 feet away was a thick jungle.

The rear of the property had the thickest jungle she had ever seen. She knew there was a creek somewhere behind that wall of brush and trees. As Lois was inspecting the dense wall, she noticed an old well-worn trail. The trail appeared to come through the center of her yard before it was put in. The trail seemed to just stop at the wall of thick vegetation. She had gone hiking her whole life and she knew a walking trail when she saw one, and this one was very old and well-used. This required closer investigation.

Much to Lois's surprise when she knelt down and looked under the jungle wall, she could see that the trail did indeed go under the wall. That part of the thick underbrush seemed to be thinner and not actually woven into the brush, but it looked like it was leaning against the wall, almost like a door. Lois went into the shed, grabbed her gloves and branch loppers, and headed back to the wall. It took a bit of close inspection to find how the wall was held in place. Lois found that three thick branches were pushed through the side of the loose wall into the thicker side. One branch on top, one in the middle, and one on the bottom seemed to be all that held the wall in place, so Lois cut all three and stepped back.

The wall section immediately dropped when Lois cut the three branches. She knew she had figured it out, and after a bit of pulling, the wall opened enough she could look inside. To her amazement, there was a large clear pond in the center of a clearing, inside the thick jungle. The pond was a good 100 feet across and surrounded my grass, Randomly spread throughout the grass were a few dozen areas of moss that looked somewhat like beds. She could see the bottom of the pond, which appeared to be only 5 or 6 feet deep and was sandy. When Lois looked at the moss bedlike areas, they did appear to have been slept in. She guessed this was a favorite place for the local deer. With the nice grass, water, and nearly impenetrable wall, this was a perfect, and very safe place for the deer. Lois was thinking how wonderful it would be if she and the deer could get along.

After inspecting the pool and surrounding jungle wall, Lois found a couple of trails into the pool, that were not as worn as the one in her back yard. Her guess was that the construction company closed off this pool because it wasn't on community property. She was now sure the deer could easily get into the pool, so she devised a plan to keep the pond to herself. After she was satisfied her plan could work, Lois went back to her shed and retrieving her rake and a shovel. She used the rake and shovel to hold the wall closed like the branches she cut had before. With the secret door to the pool closed, Lois headed into the house to make a few calls, to pull off her plan. The first thing Lois needed was a path down to the pool, which she could walk on.

# 4

## SECRET MUSIC COTTAGE

The first thing Lois needed to do before starting to work by the hidden pool, was to build a patio in the backyard so that she could entertain, and still keep her pool secret. After drawing up simple plans, Lois had an idea of what she was going to do. She needed a big entertainment area that would keep visitors away from her secret place. She called and ordered all the materials she would need. Once the materials were delivered Lois set to work. She started by leveling the area for the patio, spread the gravel, then the sand was raked over the gravel. Once the sand was smooth, she began laying the pavers. Once Lois had all the pavers set, she used a broom to spread more sand between the pavers to prevent them from moving. After the patio was ready Lois began adding the blocks for the fire circle, tables, benches, and finally the barbecue.

She designed the patio to go right up to the movable wall, then Lois placed two rolling carts in front of the area, to keep it hidden. Once the patio was complete, Lois began the long process of laying the pavers to create a path through the wall down toward the flat spot by the pool she had chosen. The total distance to the flat spot from the wall was 75 feet. The blocks were 12 inches by 12 inches, and the path was 4 feet wide. That meant she needed 300 pavers just for the path, plus she had to level it out a bit before she could lay the pavers. Ok, this was going to take longer than she imagined, she thought as she began carrying the 20-pound pavers two at a time. OH, she thought again, and when she was done with the path, she had to level and lay pavers where she was going to build her music room.

Retiring early has its advantages when you need lots of time to build a secret getaway. After having the pavers delivered, it took Lois 2 weeks to complete the path, level the building spot, and then lay the pavers for the music cottage floor. Next, she had to order the materials for the music cottage. Her design would be a 12-foot by 12-foot building with cinderblock walls that came up to a 4-foot height, then she would use glass blocks for the next 4 feet. This would allow plenty of natural light, provide great protection from Florida storms, and she would be able to carry the building materials herself, so no one would find out her secret. Her roof would use 14-foot-long boards which she could carry, and she would be using tiles for the roof. Tiles are easier to carry than heavy asphalt shingles, and much easier to install for one person.

Lois was grateful the materials for the cottage took longer than expected because it gave her a chance to rest up after laying all the pavers. While she was resting, she studied masonry, so she would be able to build her walls. She was glad she was able to take the time to study, because working with brick and concrete is not too complicated, but requires, carrying cinderblocks, mixing concrete, plus using a string line to build it straight and flat.

Once the materials arrived, Lois spent a week building the

wood frame for the cottage, then it took 3 weeks to build the walls. When she was done with the walls, Lois stood back and was amazed she was able to build something when she had never used tools before. Now it was time to build the roof. When Lois built the walls, she set all the roof brackets into the concrete to add strength. She brought the 14-foot roof rafters down to the cottage and one by one lifted them into the roof brackets. Once the rafters were attached, Lois added the cross boards that the roof tiles attached to. After three days of carrying roof tiles, 2 at a time, and attaching them to the roof, the cottage was ready for its large sliding doors. Lois wanted plenty of fresh air, so the whole front of the cottage opened up completely. By opening the doors fully and sliding them back into the side wall the front could be opened to the full width of the cottage.

Once Lois had the doors installed the cottage could finally be closed and locked, which meant it was time for the finishing touches, like lights, furniture, a day bed, and her most important addition, the white baby grand piano. Lois always dreamed of having a white baby grand piano but never had the room. After seeing the hidden pool, she knew what she wanted to do. Lois made the room, then went and bought her dream piano. The biggest obstacle to the piano was getting it to the cottage, by herself.

She was going to do everything in her power to prevent anyone from finding out about the pool and her cottage. After some research, Lois found a low-to-the-ground electric flatbed cart they used in a brick factory, that could carry the weight of the piano, and had it delivered. Her plan was to use the cart to carry the piano to the cottage. Once there she would keep the piano on the cart inside the cottage, so she could move the piano out the doors anytime she wanted. The cart was big enough to hold the piano and her piano bench, so she could move it around and easily play anywhere. After 2 months' work, Lois's cottage was complete and had a brand-new white baby grand piano sitting inside. It was close to the end of summer, and still plenty warm at night. Lois fully opened the two front doors and prepared to play for the first time.

## 5
---

# UNSEEN AUDIENCE AT THE FIRST RECITAL

Lois picked a classical song made especially for the piano in a solo concert. It was loud and it would last for almost an hour. It had been a while since she played, and she had built up a massive amount of stress and emotions since the loss of her husband, she needed to get out. This piece always brought her emotions to their peak and usually after an hour, she was able to bleed all the stress out through her music. For the next hour, Lois pounded her baby grand piano like her life depended on it. In a way it did, because getting rid of the pain was the beginning of her new life. When she hit the last note, with tear-filled eyes, her heart opened and sent her stress to heaven where her husband could hold it for her, so she could move on. Lois lay her head on the keyboard and softly wept, then fell into a light asleep, unaware her emotional piano playing had drawn an audience.

Gu had watched the new hairless one that lived in the box outside their pool grotto, build a smaller box by their pool. He was angry and thinking about breaking the new box apart, so the hairless one would leave their pool until the hairless one brought a wonderful-sounding little box out of the big box and put it pool side. The hairless one made the most wonderful sounds come out of the small box. Gu listened to the sound and watched the hairless one show deep emotions while it made the sounds. The other hairless one's box across the tracks made good sounds, but this hairless one made sounds that made Gu feel sometimes happy then sometimes sad. Gu wished the hairless one would continue playing but it fell asleep. Gu would not break the hairless one's box if it would make those sounds more, it thought.

Over the next month, Lois would go to the pool in the morning and have an apple with her tea while she played. In the evening once it cooled a bit, she headed back out to play until the stars showed through the tree canopy. Sometimes Lois sings along with her piano. When singing she sometimes thinks she hears sounds in the dense jungle surrounding the pool. It almost sounds like they are trying to repeat her words in the song but in a whisper. Lois isn't worried about animals or people because she always carries bear spray outside. The community is called Bear Creek for a reason. There are bears around the area. Lois is confident the bears will stay away, but having the spray makes her feel safe. And if it works on a bear it will work on a bad guy, she always said.

One morning Lois was in a hurry and didn't eat her apple and accidentally left it on the table that sat by the piano on the deck. She moved the piano back into the cottage and closed it up but left the apple. As she was leaving, Lois saw her apple she hadn't eaten, sitting on the table, and against better judgment she left it. She knew with bears around it was never a good idea to leave food out, which is why the music cottage does not have a refrigerator or any food inside that might attract them. When Lois returned that night to play in the evening, she noticed the apple was gone, and immediately began worrying about bears. That's when she saw a flower sitting where the apple had been that morning.

Lois approached the table and saw that the flower was real. The flower looked freshly picked and unlike any flower she had ever seen. It looked somewhat like an orchid, but the size was huge, and the color was a brilliant red. The flower was bigger than a dinner plate, and the red color was so bright it was simply unbelievable. OK, she thought, someone must have come through a deer trail and traded my apple for this fantastic flower. I think I got the better of the deals she said as she picked up the flower and smelled it. The smell was heavenly. It was a cross between berries and vanilla. Lois smelled the flower for a few Moments, then held it up and exclaimed a loud thank you. Lois gave it another smell, then sat to play for her evening calming session. This time she played as if she had an audience. As Lois began playing, her audience gathered to listen from the cover of the thick brush around the pool. She would be shocked if she knew who had been watching and listening since she arrived.

## 6

## APPLES TRADED FOR FLOWERS AND GLASS TRINKETS

The next morning after Lois discovered the incredible flower, she headed to the local fruit stand for a box of apples. If her music-loving, apple-trading guests wanted to trade flowers for apples she was all in. After she brought the flower into the house, she discovered it was actually a bromeliad flower, not an orchid. A bromeliad flower is called an air plant and doesn't need soil. It grows on trees and rocks. This meant the flower was not just incredibly beautiful, it was still alive. Lois had taken it to the fruit stand to see if anyone there could identify it. Not one person there had ever seen one like it and guessed it was from the deep Florida jungle. One of the farmers suggested her best bet was to go to the university, to see if anyone in the horticulture department could identify if.

With a box of apples, and more questions than she had when she started, Lois headed home. Her plan was that after having her tea and leaving a couple of apples to see if her admirers would leave another flower. Once she finished playing and left her treats for trade, Lois would head to the college and see if anyone there could give her an idea of what this beautiful flower is. It was two weeks before college started, but the farmer said the agricultural department was there year-round because of the plants and animals that needed care.

Lois walked down to the pool with a few apples and her tea. As usual, she played for an hour. Interestingly again when she sang, she would swear it sounded like someone was trying to mimic her words. It was quiet but she would swear she could hear it and it seemed to be more than one voice. If someone asked her why she was curious but not scared, she wouldn't be able to answer. For some reason the sounds she heard, felt innocent, and non-threatening. It was almost like non-English-speaking kids were singing along with her piano. It only happened when she sang and played at the same time. She would have to try some kid's songs and nursery rhymes next time. Now she was wondering if these sounds were from kids that lived in the swamp around the area and never went to school. She had seen specials about swamp people, and since the senior community is built way out in the middle of nothing, maybe we intruded on their homestead, she wondered.

It took Lois almost 20 minutes to find someone in the college's agricultural department. She found them in the green houses watering, and one by one asked if they had an idea what her flower was. Finally, she found the head Professor in his office, but he had never even seen a bromeliad flower so big or brilliant in color. After checking all the books in his office, he declared he was stumped.

The head Professor was putting the last book back on the shelf when he suddenly turned and exclaimed, "Oh, my gracious, it's a living fossil!"

"What?" said Lois. "What do you mean it's a living fossil?" She asked.

The Professor said, "At first, I thought this was a hybrid of a current flower, but there was no cross-reference flower that was even close because this flower has a small set of vestigial roots, which means it is the missing link to the bromeliads of today. This flower still has small roots, whereas the modern ones evolved away from them, millions of years ago, and only get nutrients from the water and trees. This one can be planted in soil as well as live off air."

"So, what does that really mean Professor?" asked Lois.

"It means that this is a completely new species or a holdover from prehistoric days, but either way is worth a fortune to a collector, plant breeder, or even a museum," said the Professor.

"Why is a plant worth a fortune, and how much is a fortune while we're asking questions?" asked Lois.

"A plant like that is worth a fortune because it is so incredibly rare, and as for how much is it worth? "Well, that question would take some research to answer," said the Professor.

"I am not sure if I want a roundabout figure right now, for the flower, or wait until you get a firm price, and fantasize about a figure," said Lois.

"Actually, it could easily be worth in the hundreds of thousands of dollars to the right collector," said the Professor. "If you find any more of these or even other types, you would be able to sell those too.:

"Do you mean to tell me I can sell every one of these flowers I can find, and for possibly hundreds of thousands of dollars each?" asked Lois.

"That is unless is unless you find a patch with millions of these flowers, then the price would drop, but up until such time as the rareness of these flowers makes them valuable to certain individuals and companies," the Professor said.

"Professor, how about you keep this flower while you do your research? Also, I would like to offer you a deal. We could be 50 / 50 partners. I will find the flowers, and you will find buyers, if that sounds like a deal to you, let's shake on it and draw up a quick agreement," Lois said.

"You do realize you will be losing a great deal of money if you make this agreement with me, don't you," asked the Professor. "Oh, and I am all for it if you are so crazy."

"I mean it, Professor. I have too much to worry about without needing to add plant selling to the list," said Lois. "You doing your part is worth it to me to avoid the stress."

"You have a deal," said the Professor as they shook hands. "Let's draw up a quick contract and exchange personal information, then you can head out and find more flowers."

Over the next few weeks, Lois played her piano by the pool and every morning she left a few apples. Every evening there were a few gifts in trade for the apples. Sometimes there was a flower like the first and there were a couple of other types of flowers the Professor was excited about. Most of the time the trades for the apples were things other than flowers. The traders left plain old run-of-the-mill rocks and funny-shaped sticks. Other times they left pretty rocks and smooth colored glass.

Lois used the rocks they left as decorations around the cottage deck where she played the piano. The sticks she left in a pile by the fire pit in the event she made a fire. The colored glass she put on the shelves on the outside and inside of the cottage. Lois built shelves on the outside walls of the cottage for plants to sit on and thought of putting the pretty colored glass on them. Lois loved how beautiful it looked when sun beams hit the glass, and the cottage looked plain. She wasn't sure where they found all this pretty glass. Some were the size of grapes, and some were the size of plums. None of the glass was thin or sharp, so she was not sure where it came from, but it looked pretty, so she used it to make sparkles around her place.

One morning 3 weeks after her first meeting with the Professor, she had a phone message from him asking her to come to his office. She had dropped off 9 other flowers that her music and apple admirers had left at his office over the 3 weeks since. He did not leave any specific information, except to meet him, so she was beside herself wondering, until she got to his office and heard the news. Over the 3 weeks, Lois brought the Professor 10 plants total, and there were 3 different varieties. The Professor suggested she sit before they talked.

"It appears the rareness of those plants is a bigger deal than I had imagined," started the Professor. "Three of the collectors and 4 plant breeders had a bidding war which drove the price to a guaranteed $200,000 for each of these first 10 plants, and $100,000 a plant afterward if they can have the first choice.

"I told them no already because I think it is not a good idea, but they asked if there was any way you would share where you found these flowers, so they could do a better search for more varieties. They said they would still pay $100,000 for every new variety."

"Let me think about letting them search, because right now I am trying to get used to the thought you and I each now have one million dollars for 10 plants," said Lois putting her head into her hands.

"I will let them know we have a deal on the flowers, and they will have to wait on a decision, about their being able to do their own searching," said the Professor, "and I will let you know when they have the funds for the flowers ready," the Professor gave her with a big smile. "Lastly, I will set up an offshore bank account, so no one knows what's happening, which is common when working in the high altitudes of private flower collectors."

Lois had no memory of the drive home. Her thoughts were about the amount of money these people would pay for flowers. I guess it's all about business and how much they can make on these flowers in a retail market, she thought. After she got home Lois went to the secret pool to play for a while. After the Professor's news, she would need a second cup of tea, and some relaxing music to soothe her soul.

# 7

## APPLE THIEF'S IDENTIFIED

When Lois got to the cottage, she saw a few trades on the table. After bringing her piano out to play, she glanced at the table. On the trade table was another beautiful flower, which would make her more money, and a couple of those pieces of pretty glass they liked to trade. Now that she knew what the flowers were worth, *maybe, just maybe* she thought, *if I could yell out for them to bring more flowers, maybe they would.*

Lois usually doesn't come down to the pool during midday and was happy with the way the sunlight made the glass trinkets shine and reflect light. She had been playing her piano for almost 10 minutes when she heard a noise coming from the thick brush from the other side of the pool. Lois designed the cottage to be bearproof, so she felt safe. Lois watched closely to see if it was a bear, which would mean she would run like the wind to the cottage and lock the door.

The thick brush began to part, and Lois saw a small hairy hand slowly pushing through, then the whole body came completely through and stood in plain view. Her first thought was it was a baby bear, then it began to walk towards her, and she realized it was some sort of monkey or ape. The odd thing was it didn't walk like an ape or monkey, it walked upright like a human. As the creature walked slowly around the pool Lois realized she wasn't afraid at all. She is normally a cautious person even when meeting new dogs, but for some reason, she felt completely at ease with this small creature walking towards her. It was then she saw it was carrying a flower in its little hands. As the small creature approached, Lois began hearing little grunts and chirps, from the thick brush. Not one or two spots but a dozen or more.

The look on the little creature's face was as easy to read as a child. A child with a fur-covered face. Aside from the hair, the little creature looked human enough if it were hairless, you could easily mistake it for a human child's face. The creature had begun walking slower, holding its head lower, and holding the flower out further. Obviously, the creature slowed down because it was scared. The poor little thing was holding its head low to hide its eyes, and not make eye contact with her. The noise from the brush around the pool was getting a bit louder as the little creature approached, but it didn't seem to be frantic sounding, so if it was its own kind, they weren't acting too worried. *Yet,* she thought, she would stay vigilant, and she also had her bear spray at her side just in case.

The little creature walked to the trade table, put the flower onto it, turned to Lois, and held out both hands as if it were asking for or expecting something. Then it dawned on her, that the little thing wanted an apple. Lois looked at the little thing, slowly got to her feet, and walked backward into the cottage where the apple box was. The whole time as she walked into and out of the cottage she kept her eyes on the little creature, who had yet to move since it put the flower on the table. Lois picked up two apples and slowly walked back outside. She paused next to her piano, still a bit unsure, but the look on the face of that little creature told her she was safe. Lois stepped up to the little creature who still had its hands held out and placed both apples into its palms. The little thing looked at the apples in its hands, then up at Lois and grinned. Without hesitation, the little creature hugged Lois's leg, walked over to her piano, sat down by her bench, and began eating its first apple.

Lois was so stunned, she walked over to the piano, sat down on the bench, and started playing. The little creature snuggled up to her leg as she played, ate its apples, and made humming and chirping noises while she played. Lois was feeling like she was in a surreal dream. Here she was playing the piano by a secret pool, with a little monkey ape thing snuggling her leg, thinking it couldn't get any stranger, when it suddenly got much weirder.

While she was playing, more little hands poked through the thick brush, followed by the full bodies of 6 more little hairy creatures like the one eating her apples, and snuggling her leg. Lois was now so shocked, that she believed she was in a dream. A very strange and realistic dream to be sure. These new little hairy creatures were also carrying things in their hands as they walked around the pool towards Lois. As with the little one at her side, each of the 6 new ones stopped at the table, deposited something, and held their hands out. At this point, Lois let out a little giggle. She wasn't sure if it was because she was scared, or that the sight of 6 little hairy ape things, standing quietly holding their hands out for apples, was indeed so cute she giggled.

Lois looked down at her furry friend at her feet, who was now looking up at her, and she smiled at it, ruffled its furry little head, and then stood and walked to get more apples. This time Lois brought the whole box and was glad she bought the big one because, from the looks of these cuties, she would be needing plenty.

When she returned to the trading table and the 12 waiting hands, she placed the box on the table and began placing 2 apples into the hands of each of the little ones. As each one received their apples. They looked up at Lois, smiled, bowed their heads, and went and sat by the piano with their friend. After the last little one walked to the piano and sat down, they all looked at her as if begging her to come back and play while they ate. Lois gave a big sigh, shook her head in disbelief, and walked to her piano to give her first monkey recital. While playing she heard the little ones humming and watched in fascination as they swayed to the music. From the way they are reacting to her playing, it had been them listening from the jungle, while she played, that is until today. Lois was deep in thought while she was playing when the little ones turned at once and stared into the brush.

# 8

## 10-FOOT-TALL SCARE

Lois was enjoying the little ones but still thinking how super strange it was when she heard a weird noise. It wasn't so much that Lois heard a noise, but she felt it. It was like all the wind moved in the pool area, yet there wasn't a sound to be heard. The little ones stopped eating, stopped moving, lowered their heads, and seemed nervous when Lois heard branches moving and breaking across the pool to her right. This wasn't a twig snapping sound, but big branches being moved and broken with great ease like a bulldozer knocking trees over. The new visitor was coming through the brush one hand first, just like the 7 little fur-covered creatures at her feet. The only difference was this hand was almost as big by itself, as one of the little ones eating an apple. Then the whole body came through, and Lois almost fainted.

This animal was huge. It was at least 10 feet tall and bigger than any ape she had ever seen. It was the biggest animal she had ever seen in fact. Its appearance was similar to that of a giant ape, with a more human-like face, and it even stood straight like a human. The huge ape thing paused after entering the pool grotto, looked around the pool area, looked at the little ones around Lois, looked at Lois in the eyes, then tilted its great head back and gave an incredibly loud and long call. Once it finished the call, it looked Lois in the eyes again, gave her a big smile, bowed its head, turned, and returned to the dense jungle.

Once the giant left the pool grotto, the little ones started chirping and acting excitedly. As the little ones were chirping, Lois started hearing more sounds coming from the jungle. At this point, there wasn't anything that could surprise Lois after seeing that huge ape thing, or so she thought as almost a dozen more of the hairy ape things came out of the jungle. These were bigger than the little ones sitting around her piano, but much smaller than the big ones that just left. Lois decided that the big one was the leader, the little ones were the young, and the new ones must be the females. As they approached, Lois could see they all carried something in their hands.

One by one the new visitors placed their trade gifts on the table and stood with their hands open, like the smaller ones did. At least Lois didn't have any difficulty understanding their meaning now. The notion that food talks clearly to these beings will be something she will remember. These females were all around 7 feet tall and like the small ones, they had a face that was closer to human than ape shape. Lois actually felt safe with all these huge beings. She knew if they had wanted to hurt her, they would have already done it, so she got up and walked to the trade table.

Lois gave each of the females 4 apples apiece, because of their size. She thought again how grateful she bought a big box of apples, as the last female took her apples and went to sit by the little ones. It was obvious from their subtle hints that the females also wanted her to play the piano while they ate their apples. No one would believe what was happening to her, and Lois wasn't sure if it was really happening herself. She knew for sure, there was no way she could tell a soul for fear they would hurt these gentle creatures. For the next 2 hours, Lois played the piano for her new friends. A few of the little ones fell asleep curled up in a ball around her piano, and the rest had climbed into the laps of what she assumed were their mothers and fell asleep. Lois stopped playing and looked around at her new friends. Most had been sitting with their eyes closed, rocking to the music. Now as Lois stood to put the piano away the females also stood, gathered their young, and one by one walked slowly by her and touched her gently on her shoulder, bowed their heads, and walked back into the dense jungle.

Lois watched the last of the gentle beings disappear, took a deep breath, put the piano away, and locked up the cottage. Tomorrow she would need to make a run to the fruit stand and get a few boxes of apples, she thought. Before she went up to the house, she looked at the trade table to see what the newest trinkets and flowers were bringing. Much to her pleasure there were a few more flowers, and one appeared to be a new species. Looks like she was going to be able to afford the apples, but obviously she couldn't allow the college to come looking for where those flowers were growing. Lois was sure the looks of her current flower gatherers might upset the college experts. The females really loaded the table when they came. The table now held a few weird-shaped sticks, some plain rocks, and a bunch more of the pretty colored glass they seemed to like so much. Lois put all the trade gifts away and then went home to sleep. Her world had taken a very strange turn.

# 9

## MUSIC SOOTHES THE SAVAGE BEASTS

Lois woke early and was at the fruit stand by 6 AM. Knowing she had some big eaters, she bought three boxes of apples, one box of bananas, and a large box of mixed nuts because she'd read monkeys and apes liked nuts, so she gave them a shot. When she got home, she loaded the boxes of fruit and nuts onto a hand truck and headed down to the secret pool.

She didn't know what to expect after yesterday's weirdness, so when Lois saw the hairy visitors already there, she wasn't all that surprised. They were all spread around the pool laying on the bed-shaped moss. Some of the females were sleeping together and others had a young one with them. When they saw her a chorus of chirps erupted around the pool. Some of the young ones got excited and were jumping up and down. The females were keeping the little ones calm, and holding on to them, as Lois reached the trade table. Lois unloaded the nuts, the bananas, and one box of apples, then took the rest over to the cottage. The whole time Lois was unloading the boxes and opening up the cottage to roll out the piano not one of the little ones or females left their nest.

Even after Lois had laid out the apples, bananas, and nuts, not one of the little ones or females moved. Finally, Lois looked at the lot of them, bowed her head, passed her hands over the food, and waved them to come. When that didn't work, she sat down at the piano and began playing soft morning wake-up music. Slowly, one by one, they came up to the table, picked up either an apple, banana, or a handful of nuts, and sat to listen. After 10 or 15 minutes, Lois heard a loud rustling in the dense jungle moving towards the pool. This time she wasn't surprised when a 10-foot-tall ape thing lumbered into the pool grotto, stopped, and stared at the sight. When it walked around the pool towards Lois, she began to feel slightly nervous. When it was 10 feet away looking down at the trade table, she was sure her heart was going to stop. When it picked up a single banana, turned to look at her, and smiled, she nearly burst out laughing, it was so funny.

Here she was terrified of a 10-foot-tall man-ape when it gently picked up a banana in its huge hand, then turned and smiled at her. She was ready for a deep growl or to have it try to eat her, and it simply picked up a banana, smiled, and then sat to listen to piano music in a secret jungle grotto. As terrifying as it was, it was also so absolutely weird that she wanted to laugh. There is no way anyone would ever believe this was happening. She was going to have to get a movie camera to record this. Although, at this point, until she could figure out how to keep them safe, it was best to keep the existence of these beings secret. It was also imperative that she determine what it was these creatures were before she went too far. If prehistoric flowers can exist in this Florida swamp, then maybe a prehistoric ape can also. In fact, she thought, maybe these are what the Native Americans call Sasquatch. Looks like I will be heading to college again, but this time to the paleontology department, to look up extinct primitive ape species.

With a plan in place, Lois played her heart out for the intently listening furry friends. As she played Lois noticed the music seemed to calm them. The huge male leader had finished his single banana and was laying back with his eyes closed listening to her music. She would swear he had a smile on his face too. The young ones also were laying calmly listening to her play, and sometimes they hummed along as she played, which gave her an idea. Lois started playing simple kids' songs with simple tunes and words. Once she played a kid's song, the little ones would perk up and move with the music. A couple of young ones tried copying her words when Lois played and sang 'Jack and Jill went up the hill."

Lois began playing the kids' songs 4 or 5 times in a row, so they could learn the tune and maybe the words. To balance things out she would then play 4 or 5 classical songs, which seemed to be their favorite music, except for the nursery rhymes that is.

If the little ones were trying to speak, maybe she could try to teach them. They are very smart, seem to have a simple sign language, and certain sounds they make seem to mean something especially when the big male makes it, so why not try teaching words she thought. After she finished today, she would search out the lady she met last month by the clubhouse, who used to be a teacher. She must have an idea of what books she could use to teach these hairy toddlers. Which brings up a good point. What excuse does she use for needing to teach she wondered? Well, she does have her grandkids she can always use as an excuse, she decided.

The furry audience was relaxed and after an hour two of the females got up while she played and left the grotto. When they came back, they were each carrying a woven basket the size of a laundry basket. They walked to the trade table and placed the baskets on the table, turned to Lois, bowed, and then left the grotto once more. Once they had set the baskets down and left, the other females stood, bowed, and walked out of the grotto. One by one the 7 little ones came up to Lois, smiled up at her, gave her a hug, then turned and followed the females out. Lastly, the big male stood. All 10 feet of massive, muscular, hairy giant stood over 5-foot-5-inch Lois. He bent down to look at her, squinted his eyes to look at her closely, and then ever so slowly a grin appeared on his lips, followed by a full-on smile, and if she were to place money on it, he laughed a bit. Then he stood to full height, gently placed a huge finger on her shoulder, and gave the deepest short grunt she had ever heard, turned, and walked out of the grotto.

There will never be another Moment in her life that Lois will remember more than having an almost 1200-pound, 10-foot-tall animal, gently touch her. The exhilaration, fear, and excitement were beyond belief. After sitting for another 10 minutes Lois began packing things away. After putting the piano in the cottage, she went to the trade table to get the food to lock it away. When she looked at the trade table, she was surprised that they each only took one piece of fruit or banana, especially the big male. Obviously, they weren't hungry, but for a wild animal to be so controlled that they limit themselves to one piece was amazing, she thought. After locking up the fruit Lois looked into the baskets the 2 females brought.

As she looked at the baskets it suddenly dawned on her that the females had brought stuff in baskets, not their bare hands. These baskets looked handmade, and she was now wondering where they got them, because in no way could wild animals, no matter how nice they were, make a woven basket. Not even a chimp can weave, she thought. They were nice, and eventually, Lois believed they had stolen them from somewhere. No matter, because the baskets each had a mixture of sticks, stones, a few more flowers, and a bunch more of that pretty glass. Thank goodness for those flowers. She wasn't really hurting for money, but these new hairy friends could easily eat her out of house and home, so the flower money would be very handy.

Her outside shelves were filling, so it looked like Lois was going to need to put some of that glass on the inside cottage shelves too. Maybe she would get a wooden box to hold the glass until she figured out something she could make with such pretty glass. It was a bit too thick for stained glass work, but maybe she could drill some and make necklaces for her granddaughters. After all the new trinkets were put away Lois went up to the house for lunch, and a trip to the college's paleontology department.

## 10

# FINDING OUT WHAT HER
# FRIENDS ARE

The college paleontology department was not open, but the department head was in her office doing work, and asked Lois to come in to talk. Lois's plan was to ask if there was any information on recent sightings of huge ape things because she was doing research on a book. The department head turned out to be a lady approximately Lois's age, who was in her office cleaning out her desk. She was retiring and planning on living a life of leisure, and no more lectures. Lois and the Professor talked about her upcoming retirement, and Lois explained her situation as well, having just retired herself. When it finally got to the part of why Lois was there, a thought began to brew in Lois's head, so she started asking the Professor personal questions.

The Professor was taken aback by the change and asked why all of a sudden, she was being grilled. Lois explained she had found an interesting and possibly new primate species, but wanted the Professor to give her word she would not tell a soul. Lois told the Professor she would tell her everything about the new species, then introduce her to them, if the Professor gave her word that she would not say a thing to anyone.

The Professor's eyes widened with the words 'introduce you to them,' and looked at Lois with a thousand questions on her mind, but stayed silent, so Lois could continue.

Lois told the Professor the whole story, from the first sounds she heard to the little guy asking for an apple, all the little ones and females, and then the big male. Lois wasn't sure if the Professor took a breath during her description of the huge male. She told of the ape things trading for fruit, then listening to the music. When Lois stopped talking, the Professor was staring wide-eyed, open-mouthed, and breathing in quick shallow breaths.

Finally, the Professor looked at Lois and asked, "are you pulling my leg, did someone here put you up to this because I was retiring and wanted to tease me? Tell me the truth, are you serious?"

"I promise, everything I have said is true, and I am prepared to bring you there right now to meet them," said Lois. "I guess coming to see them is better than trying to find them in a book any day."

"Until I see them for myself, I will consider this an interesting drive into Ormond Beach and to be honest I always wanted to check out The Bear Creek Senior community for myself," said the Professor.

Lois said, "If you are ready right now, let's head to my place, make a couple of cups of tea, walk down to the grotto, and just maybe blow your Professor mind."

"Lois," said the Professor, "I am more ready now than ever, and if this is real, my life will definitely be complete," said the Professor, as she gathered her purse, shut off the light, and followed Lois to her car.

Once they reached Lois's place, they made tea and went out

the back door, and as they approached the hidden entrance, Lois stopped and asked the Professor if she had changed her mind and if not, was she ready.

The professor looked at Lois and said, "If this is real there is no way to prepare for it, so lead the way."

When they walked down the path to the cottage Lois saw a few little ones and some females acting as babysitters. When the Professor's eyes adjusted to the light and she saw the hairy creatures were indeed there, she let out a gasp, grabbed Lois's hand, and held tight. Once they got to the cottage, Lois peeled the Professor's hand off hers and stepped onto the cottage deck. Lois opened the cottage door. Ran the electric cart with the piano outside and sat down to play. Once she sat to play the young ones stood and slowly made their way to the Professor, who was standing by the trade table.

"This is unbelievable. These have to be Gigantopithecus, but they can't be because they were supposed to have gone extinct over a million years ago," said the Professor, as she stood in the middle of the young ones while the Moms and other females stood to the side watching. "If these are the Gigantopithecus, then they have evolved in the last million years plus, to walk upright like humans. I would be willing to bet that these are what people have been calling Sasquatch for years."

As Lois began playing, the little ones gently held the Professor's hands and led her to a mossy spot where they sat down and snuggled with her. Lois saw the Professor's face as she was cuddling the little ones, and the look of pure love and joy on her face was precious. The little ones were checking the Professor out as well. Lois has red hair, and the Professor has gray hair, which the little ones seem to be so fascinated by, that they wouldn't leave it alone. The Professor didn't seem to mind one little bit from the look on her face.

The Professor looked at Lois and said, "Is there any chance we can sleep here tonight? This is the most wonderful thing that has ever happened to me."

"I wanted to do the same thing until I realized they all seem to leave for the night, and then I would be alone with the bears and snakes," said Lois.

"That is good information to have, next time I feel like sleeping outside in Florida," said the Professor faking a scared look.

The Sasquatch females stood one by one and gathered the little ones to leave. The little ones all hugged the Professor one more time before they left.

After the Sasquatch left, Lois and the Professor departed the grotto also. The Professor told Lois she was going to be buying there as soon as she could arrange the purchase, and that there was no way Lois could keep her away from these precious beings because they needed to be protected. Lois agreed and they began making plans to take care of the Sasquatch together. Not only did she find out what her new friends are, she found a new friend. Looks like two little old ladies, were embarked on an exciting retirement, Lois thought smiling.

# 11

## TEACHING THE SASQUATCH TO TALK

Lois asked her friend who had been a daycare teacher what the best songs to learn vocabulary for toddlers were. Her friend listed songs like *Ring Around The Rosy*, the *Hokey Pokey*, and *Head, Shoulders, Knees And Toes*, as a few of the songs she could start with to teach vocabulary. The teacher also gave her suggestions for using flash cards with pictures of natural things on them with the words, like for instance different fruits, flowers, trees, rocks, animals, a table, and even fish could help build a vocabulary of things they see and use every day.

Once Lois left her teacher friend's house, she went straight to the store to buy flashcards, picture books she could cut pictures out of, glue and colored felt pens. If she couldn't find the right flashcards, she would have to make them herself. To teach the Sasquatch how to speak, she needed to have pictures of the items that they were familiar with, so they could draw the connection to the picture, the spoken words, and the written words on the card. Pretty much, she would be teaching Sasquatch words, as they learn in preschool, the same way they teach human kids.

After picking up the teaching supplies, Lois went to the local music store and picked up new sheet music. She would make sure to pick up as many sing-along kid's songs as she could find, and a good mixture of various music styles to find out which are their favorites. Lois had not played the piano for years when she moved, and her plan was to have a secret hideaway to play and spend her retirement years. Now, she had embarked on the weirdest adventure and was grateful she opened up to the Professor, who is now her ally. Oh, what is ever going to become of this she thought as she pulled into her driveway, only to see the Professor sitting on her front step with a piece of paper and a smile.

The Professor started jumping up and down once Lois stopped the car. Turned out a salesperson for Bear Creek saw the Professor looking at brochures, and suggested they drive around and look. When they got to the street Lois's house was on, the salesperson informed her that the buyer of the first house before Lois' had decided not to buy. They did not want to live by the deep woods and bought another home in the center of the community, so the house next to Lois was now available. Although it was still 500 feet away from Lois's house, she was the first neighbor. The Professor helped carry all the teaching materials into Lois's house, and they sat down for tea, and to plan their next moves.

In between the time they spent down in the grotto with the Sasquatch, Lois, and the Professor made flash cards. The professor was a great resource for teaching even though she had been a college Professor because the principles of teaching are universal. The Professor explained that once the Sasquatch recognizes that the picture on the flashcard of a tree is the same as the word they say when they point to the tree, then they will have made a breakthrough. From then on, it was a matter of increasing the vocabulary and teaching the alphabet, and spelling.

The professor suggested using the flashcards with just the

picture first. Once the Sasquatch can relate the pictures to the correct spoken words, they will add the written words to the picture. Although it will be important to teach them the alphabet in a song at the same time, then introduce the letters. Lois was grateful she had found expert help and a nice friend in the professor.

After two weeks of training with the flashcards, the sasquatch progress was amazing, according to the professor. The Sasquatch were able to grasp the picture of an apple to the spoken word first. Lois decided to use an apple first because they were one of the Sasquatch's most favorite treats. Once they realized the connection between the words like apple, other fruits, or plants which were followed by pictures of local animals, they were able to begin to learn English. Many of the young Sasquatch were able to say words more easily. The older ones seemed to have more difficulty forming words, but their understanding was excellent. The Professor thought that their muscles were too overdeveloped or strong to learn to form new and complex shapes easily. The two ladies went into the grotto twice a day for 4 weeks, to work with the Sasquatch.

By the end of week four the Professor looked at Lois, looked at the Sasquatch laying around the pool, threw her head back, and exclaimed, "we have taught a troupe of supposedly extinct apes to speak English." Then she went on saying, "This is the greatest day in history for paleontology, yet we can't tell anyone. I mean, even if I published a professional paper, they would want proof, which would endanger our furry friends."

"OH, well, at least we are famous in our own minds," the professor added, with a deep sigh.

The future friendship between Lois and the professor looked busy but filled with excitement and lots of furry cuddles.

## 12

## INTRODUCING THE NEIGHBORS TO HER FURRY FRIENDS

One day when the professor and Lois returned to Lois's house, after having been in the grotto playing music, teaching, and enjoying time with the Sasquatch, to a neighbor sitting on her back deck. Lois was glad she had met this lady a few times and was pretty sure her secret grotto had just been found out. Lois closed the now not-so-secret door and walked to the lady.

"Um, hi," said Lois, then gave a nervous look to the professor.

"Alright ladies," the lady started. "I am pretty sure what you're doing down there isn't illegal, but it appears to be more enjoyable than sitting watching dust collect in my house since I lost my partner, and I'm begging to join the club." She added. "Oh, and my name is Nancy, by the way," she said lastly.

"I know we've met before Nancy, my name is Lois, and this wonderful lady next to me is the Professor," said Lois. If you are serious about finding out what is happening, then we need to go inside, make some tea, and talk a bit," Lois added.

The three ladies went inside, talked for two hours, and went through three pots of tea. Lois felt Nancy knew enough to make a qualified decision about whether to go down and see what they were doing or leave now and not tell a soul. Like the Professor, when Nancy was told about the Sasquatch, she remained silent, eyes wide and mouth open. Lois finished telling Nancy everything there was to know then sat back to see what her decision would be.

Nancy looked Lois in the eye and asked, "Is this for real, or have you two been drinking down behind the wall? Either way, it sounds more fun than my current life, so I'm in if you'll have me."

Lois laughed, "You're my kind of gal Nancy. Let's head outside to see if we have some furry friends visiting in the grotto for you to meet."

Lois went first, followed by the Professor, with Nancy holding onto the Professor's arm as tightly as a python. Lois heard Nancy begin to giggle nervously while they walked through the hidden door and down the path. There were indeed a few visitors, and they perked up while the ladies approached. Lois went to the cottage and drove the electric cart with the white baby grand piano on it out onto the deck. Nancy was still holding the Professor's arm while they stood by the trade table when Lois brought a basket full of fruit and nuts to put on the table. After Lois spread the food out on the table, she went to the piano and began playing.

The sasquatch recognized the new human and was being polite, for now. Once the music started the little ones began moving closer. Nancy was a bit more nervous as they approached, so the Professor held out the arm Nancy wasn't squeezing and waved for one of the smallest Sasquatch to come over to them. The little one came over; the Professor picked it up, then it snuggled in tight. Nancy drew in a deep breath, returned the sweet gaze those little sasquatch eyes were giving her, and then reached out a hand to touch a furry shoulder. The little

Sasquatch smiled at Nancy and raised both arms out to her asking to be picked up.

Nancy was hesitating, so the Professor gently handed the Sasquatch to Nancy. Once in Nancy's arms, the baby Sasquatch wrapped its arms around her neck and gave the longest hug Nancy had ever had. The Professor suggested Nancy either sit or lay in a moss and relax while Lois played. Within 5 minutes, Nancy was snuggling 4 little baby Sasquatch on a flat moss bed and was in pure heaven. The little fur balls loved snuggling Nancy, then wrestling each other all the time touching her, like puppies do. Lois and the Professor had been the wrestling mat for these playful little ones many times and smiled at Nancy and her new friends.

By the time the Sasquatch left the grotto, Nancy was almost napping herself. The Professor helped Nancy out of the moss bed, then the ladies put things away and headed out of the grotto themselves. Lois suggested they go inside to make some concrete plans if they were going to work together and help these Sasquatch.

The ladies came up with a plan knowing they needed more help if they were going to be able to help all the Sasquatch and teach them to talk. Lois had not disclosed that she was getting money for the flowers the Sasquatch brought. She planned to bring that up once she knew she could trust them, but for now, they needed help, and she would throw the money situation at them as a huge surprise.

The plan they came up with was to sit by the pool and meet new people. They would fish about their lives, for things like, do you have grandkids, are you an animal lover, and so on until they could find another dozen animal-loving helpers. Although, calling them animals now that she knew the Sasquatch so well, didn't feel right. After a couple of weeks, they had chosen almost a dozen ladies who fit the bill, and they were sure wouldn't spill the beans about the Sasquatch.

Lois thought it would be best to have all the new ladies come over to her house, for tea on the back deck. If she had been a drinker, Lois would have served wine instead of tea, to the ladies to calm them down. Nancy and the Professor helped Lois get all the new ladies situated on the back deck and helped tell all of them the special things they were about to see. Once every lady said they were sure they were ready to see the Sasquatch, Lois opened the hidden wall, and they went into the grotto.

Lois, Nancy, and the Professor had spent a full week explaining to the Sasquatch that they were going to be bringing in more ladies to help. Once the females understood, they became excited. One female Sasquatch mother of two, was able to let them know she was happy for the help, because she needed more sleep, with raising two babies. The young Sasquatch that understood there were going to be more humans to cuddle, also became excited.

Much to Lois, Nancy, and the Professor's surprise, the Sasquatch decided to take advantage of all the senior lady Sasquatch babysitters, that there were new females there with new babies. Apparently, the Sasquatch had been teaching English to Sasquatch, from the surrounding area, and once some of the Moms understood, babysitting at the grotto, they came as well. It all worked out because usually there were only about 6 young Sasquatch. Today there were over a dozen, and the new ladies couldn't have been happier once they had a furry bundle in their laps.

Two hours later the sasquatch Moms began collecting their young. Each Mom walked up to the lady holding their young, knelt down, bowed, and said the best thank you they could for what little teaching they had received. These Sasquatch children learn as fast as human kids, and the Moms learn almost as fast.

After the Sasquatch had left, Lois put the piano away and led the ladies out of the grotto.

The ladies had a sit-down talk by the deck and another cup of tea. Every woman said that was the single greatest time of their lives and wanted to do it for the rest of their lives. It looked like Lois had found a great core group of friends, and helpers. The group set about the task of making plans and a schedule, so those that needed a rest, or a vacation could take it and not mess up the schedule. It was decided to search for other helpers from around Bear Creek over the next few weeks, and always keep their eyes and ears open for more in the future.

## 13

BABY SITTING SASQUATCH BABIES

I magine seeing grandmas holding and feeding Sasquatch babies. It is always heartwarming to see baby animals feeding. Babies of all species smile and make all sorts of cute feeding noises when they eat. Grandmas love babies of all kinds and when given a chance to hold them they take it willingly. When Lois's friends could finally be trusted they became the go-to babysitters for the Sasquatch.

If it hadn't put the Sasquatch at risk, Lois and the others would have taken pictures of all their new Sasquatch friends. They wanted pictures of themselves feeding, rocking, and cuddling the Sasquatch babies. For now, they would have to settle with the real thing.

Over the weeks and years that followed, the residents of Bear Creek and the Sasquatch lived in harmony. A few of the senior men in the community helped out. Some wanted to be grandpas so they could feed, hold, and play with the Sasquatch kids. The grandpas were considered the play toys for the Sasquatch kids. Some of the healthier grandpas gave horsey rides, and even wrestled a bit. There were healthcare professionals who gave checkups for the Sasquatch. It was a wonderful time for the humans and Sasquatch.

Every time Lois went down into the grotto, she was pleased to see numerous humans and Sasquatch spending time together. Now that many of the Sasquatch can talk, and understand English, they enjoy spending time with humans talking and learning new things. Some of the seniors read to the Sasquatch kids, and there are always a few adult Sasquatch listening as well. The Sasquatch do not have a written language, so the reading time is very special to them. The Sasquatch are very social, and since the humans are retired, they have plenty of time to socialize. The bonds the Sasquatch and humans are forming will last generations.

During the summer months, Lois made sure there was plenty of shade in the grotto. The Sasquatch helped install large solar-powered fans and lights in the grotto so that humans and Sasquatch could enjoy the grotto at night and during the warmest weather. The pool in the grotto was spring-fed, so it was always cool, which made it wonderful for Florida's hot humid days and nights. It wasn't unusual for one or two humans to be there in the middle of the night. Many older humans don't sleep a lot, so they make wonderful nighttime chaperones, so the adult Sasquatch can leave their young in the grotto, and there will always be an adult to keep a look out. Over the years the grotto took shape as a comfortable and safe place for humans and Sasquatch to live in peace.

There were now a few tables spread around the grotto, as well as more moss beds. As more humans and Sasquatch joined the grotto group, it became a bit crowded sometimes, so they wanted to begin spending time at one of the pools in the complex. There were now almost 100 humans living in the Bear Creek community who knew about and helped the Sasquatch. Almost all of them were from the section around Lois's home. One of them contacted the park manager, so Lois and a few of the others that had been working with the Sasquatch, sat down with her for a serious talk, to see if they could tell her about the Sasquatch.

Lois and the others tip-toed around actual Sasquatch talk at first, until they were certain she would not freak out. To say the manager was excited about having the Sasquatch in her community would be a gross understatement. The manager wanted to meet the sasquatch as soon as possible after the talk, so they brought her to the grotto.

Lois, the manager, and the others realized that only a few people who lived in Lois's section were not already involved with the Sasquatch. As it turned out the few people that were not involved with taking care of the Sasquatch were basically home-bound and never visited the pool. The manager knew that those people would never go to the pool in Lois's section, so it might be possible to gate off the section that Lois, the Sasquatch grotto, and the other helpers live in. The manager contacted the maintenance manager to have them come to the office immediately. Lois and the others were worried, but the manager told them to trust her.

When the maintenance manager arrived, the community manager told them she had a secret they needed to keep. She then introduced the maintenance manager as her husband.

"Yes, he is my husband, which is against company policy, so now you know you can trust me because if I mess things up for you, you can ruin my career. The best part," she added, "is he is a big Sasquatch believer, and I'm sure that not only would he keep the secret, but he would be a great asset to help."

The maintenance manager looked at his wife after what she said, and asked, "What is all this talk about Sasquatch?"

The community manager looked at her husband and said,

"These fine folks have invited us to help them take care of a Sasquatch troupe they have been working with for the last year." "That is if you have the time in your busy schedule." She gave a grin.

The look on her husband's face was hysterical. He was staring at his wife with wide eyes, open mouth, and not breathing. Then he looked at each of the others sitting around the table. No one was smiling, or making a funny face, which said, his wife was pulling his leg. After looking around the table, he sat down and muttered this has to be a dream.

"No, it's not a dream, but it is a bunch of work and fun," said Lois.

The others that came with Lois, sitting around the table agreed to work with the Sasquatch, was an experience they never could have never imagined, and they will never forget.

Lois stood, and announced, "It looks like it is time to show this pair of company employees what a Sasquatch looks like." "Follow me if you dare," she added and headed out to her golf cart.

The maintenance manager was the first to stand and declare he was ready to go. The rest of the group was smiling now knowing that all their hard work was not going to be at risk. Everyone followed Lois to her house and into the backyard. Once they were standing by the hidden movable wall in the grotto, Lois asked the two new ones if they were really ready to meet Sasquatch. The excited look on their faces was enough for Lois to open the wall.

The maintenance manager was stunned the wall opened, and exclaimed, "I have been in this backyard dozens of times, and never realized that wall moved."

"What you're going to be seeing next is a bit more impressive than a moving wall, so hold onto your hats, buckle your seatbelts, keep your partner's hand in yours, and don't scream because it is going to get a bit weird," said Lois as she stepped through the wall into the grotto.

The seniors that had been working with Lois stood back and let the managers go in next. As she entered the grotto, Lois saw there were indeed some Sasquatch already there, so she knew her new guests were going to get the full show. Gu wasn't there, and she thought it would be best if the new people met him right away, so she opened the cottage and drove the piano out onto the deck.

The Sasquatch had been looking at the newcomers but had not moved by the time Lois started playing. Once Lois started playing, the little Sasquatch started coming over. The looks on the two managers' faces were priceless. Lois was sure that both of them thought that they were being pranked. Now that some small Sasquatch were approaching them, the reality set in that they had been told the truth about them. The females also began approaching the group, so they could also meet the new people.

For the next 15 minutes, the managers were introduced to the Sasquatch, who were quite surprised that the Sasquatch could talk. After things settled down a bit and both managers were breathing normally, little Sasquatch walked up to each manager and held arms up indicating they wanted to be picked up. One of the seniors that had been helping suggested that the two managers sit, so it was more comfortable to snuggle. The managers were in heaven holding the young Sasquatch, while the adult female Sasquatch stood by smiling.

When the loud noises started coming from the thick jungle around the pool, both managers were startled and wanted to know what that noise was, and whether they were safe. Before anyone could answer, Gu broke through the dense jungle into the open. The gasps from both managers could have been heard for miles. If a heavy Sasquatch baby had not been sitting on the maintenance manager's lap he would have stood and run away, he admitted later.

While Gu walked around the pool, all 10-foot-1200 pounds of him was heading towards a very nervous pair of managers. Lois and her helpers had purposely failed to mention to the managers, Gu existed. The pair had been nervous about meeting the adult females, but that was nothing to the nervous fear they were now living as Gu walked towards them. When Gu was within 5 feet of the managers, the baby Sasquatch they were holding had stopped and looked down. Both were sitting on the ground in a moss bed with a baby sitting on their lap.

Lois stopped playing and introduced the managers to Gu. She explained they were the ones who worked here and ran the place. She said these two could block off access to their area in the community, so the Sasquatch could safely use the swimming pool without other community people who didn't know about the Sasquatch seeing them. When she was finished explaining to Gu why they were there, Lois suggested Gu greet the new people.

Gu caught on right away and noticed that the new humans were afraid of them, so had been going slow and easy, so as not to scare them. Gu is literally 1000 pounds heavier, and 4 to 5 foot taller than anyone else in the park, and when they are sitting on the ground, he seems even larger. Gu squatted down and got his huge head only a few feet away from the managers, then said boo, and began laughing loud and hard.

Both managers fell backward when he said boo, and the baby Sasquatch on their laps started laughing with Gu. The managers were quick to realize they had been teased and joined in on the laughter. Both managers stood to greet Gu properly. After the very exciting time meeting Gu, and the rest of the troupe, everyone sat for a meeting.

Lois described the plan to section off Lois's section, so the

Sasquatch could have a safer environment, be able to swim, and help the humans in the section. The maintenance manager mentioned how wonderful it would be to have the sasquatch help sometimes around the community. The female Sasquatch could easily do heavy lifting or moving that 3 grown men couldn't imagine together.

The Bear Creek manager decided that they would put a gate up to keep others out of Lois's section. Then they would explain to the other residents that this section was bought by Lois's group, and they wanted privacy. It will take a few weeks to complete, then the Sasquatch will be free to roam.

# 14

## GRANDKIDS MEET SASQUATCH

Lois had been in her new home for a year now, and the grandbabies were going to be coming soon to spend the summer, Lois had to figure out a way to introduce the girls to the Sasquatch but keep them from telling their parents until she could trust them to keep the secret. Every year Lois watched her two granddaughters for the whole summer, and this year things were a bit more complicated. After lots of hair-pulling thinking, Lois thought if she had a few stuffed ape and monkey toy animals around the house, and one of the girls made a comment about apes or monkeys, it could be explained away with 'it's a child's imagination' and all that stuff.

After a year of not seeing her granddaughters, they finally arrived, with Mom and Dad in tow. The two girls were now 5 and 7 years old and full of fire. Both were very smart, independent and without fear and definitely two clones of their grandmother, Lois thought with a loving smile.

After a year of living in Bear Creek without young kids around, it was quite a shock to have the two fireballs come flying into her home, all excited, and laughing. For what seemed like an hour the girls talked up a storm while hugging grandma. Mom and Dad brought the girls things in while Grandma was being mauled. It took a few loads back and forth from the car, to get all their stuff, because the girls would be staying for the summer. By the time Mom and Dad were done unloading the girls' things, the girls had settled down enough that Lois could say hi to them.

Lois decided not to tell her daughter and her husband about the Sasquatch until she knew if they would get upset. She knew her granddaughters were going to be in heaven once they met the Sasquatch, so her plan was to introduce the girls on this trip and decide when to tell their parents.

Lois's daughter and son-in-law left early the next morning, and after breakfast, it was time to take the granddaughters down to the grotto. Before she took them down to meet the Sasquatch, she sat them down to explain to them who and what the Sasquatch were. Lois knew the Sasquatch were going to love the girls, she just wanted to make sure the girls weren't going to be afraid. Once she told the girls that the Sasquatch looked like big monkeys, the girls became excited about meeting the monkeys.

When Lois and the girls entered the grotto, the girls saw the first Sasquatch and they started saying hello monkeys. There were a few humans also already there, and once they saw the girls, they came over to be introduced. Lois knew her granddaughters were going to have a fantastic summer. With the extra grandparents to spoil the granddaughters and the fun they would have with the Sasquatch, the girls were going to have a summer to remember.

The humans who had been in the grotto came over to meet the girls, and while they were talking, the Sasquatch kids began coming over. At first, the Sasquatch were nervous about the little humans. The young Sasquatch had never seen a human child, but they were fascinated. Lois told the Sasquatch that the girls were human kids. Human kids are like Sasquatch kids without hair she explained.

It only took 5 minutes for the Sasquatch kids and Lois's granddaughters to hit it off and go play together. Most of the Sasquatch kids spoke enough English to communicate with the girls, so they didn't have any problems. As always, kids of all species want to play and have fun, and that is what they did.

Lois's granddaughters spent the next three months playing with the Sasquatch kids. By the end of the summer, the girls had developed friendships with all the Sasquatch kids, and most of the adults. It was an important time for Lois and her granddaughters. They built trust in each other and had the best time ever playing in the grotto.

Lois and the girls explained to the Sasquatch that the girls would be going home the next day, and there were tears flowing, with lots of hugs. Once the Sasquatch understood the girls would be back, in a few months to visit they became happy again. The Sasquatch kids stayed all day with the girls, and Lois even let the girls stay in the grotto that night, to have a great sending away time.

## 15

# WHAT ARE THE GLASS TRINKETS

The three months of summer without the girls had gone by too quickly, according to Dad jokingly as he and Mom drove to Lois's house. Mom gave him the normal, 'you're a dork' look and looked out the car window again at the beautiful palm trees. She was very surprised at the number of oak and pine trees in Ormond Beach. The thick jungle forest reminded her of Washington state, except there weren't any natural palm trees in Washington.

When they got to Lois's house, she was in the kitchen making lunch for the girls. Mom, Dad, and Lois ate lunch and caught up on what had been going on these last 3 months. As Lois filled them in on what had been going on, she was wondering if she had gotten it through the heads of her granddaughters, to keep quiet about the Sasquatch. She had warned them that if they ever said a thing about the Sasquatch, she would never let them visit them again. The girls loved being with the Sasquatch enough to double promise they would never say a word. When they were done with lunch Dad went outside to collect the girls, for the trip back home.

Lois had instructed the Sasquatch to stay away for the day until the girls had been taken home by their parents. As Dad left, her nerves started to rise. All it would take for everything to go bad was for the girls to say something about the Sasquatch or for Dad to see one. Lois gave Dad the instructions to the grotto, then held her breath as Dad left.

The girls were on the cottage floor playing when Dad came down to the pool to see them. The girls had a couple of dolls each, a couple of books, and a bucket of pretty colored stones or plastic. After saying hi to the girls, and seeing they were doing fine, he went outside to relax and look around. His mother-in-law was a very handy lady. She had built this entire cottage herself a year ago and had done a great job. He especially liked the glass blocks on the upper part of the wall. The glass blocks let in plenty of natural light and looked great. Lois also included built-in shelves on the inside and outside that were great for holding plants and junk. While he was looking outside what caught his eye was how the colored glass that was decorating the cottage shelves on the outside as well as the inside, seemed to almost glow in the sunlight. Dad picked up a large red glass trinket and examined it closely.

The first thing Dad noticed about the glass was how heavy it was. Obviously, it wasn't plastic, but it seemed to be too heavy for normal glass. Maybe it was some sort of industrial glass waste he thought, as he continued examining various pieces. Interestingly enough, some of the pieces seemed to have facets like cut stones but appeared to be natural. If the facets were natural that meant these stones, weren't glass, but some sort of natural stones. It wouldn't be possible for these stones to be natural, Dad thought, because there were too many to begin with, and if they were real, they would be worth a fortune, and would not be decorating a small cottage in the middle of the jungle.

The more stones Dad looked at the more he thought they were actually real stones. What he needed to do was collect a sample of all the stone colors, types, and sizes so he could take them to a jeweler to have them tested. Dad found a basket and began putting a variety of stones in it. He picked the largest, red, green, blue, and clear stones he could find, and added a bunch of the smaller stones and what he assumed were fake pearls. His basket was beginning to get heavy, and it didn't have that many stones in it, which made him again think that these were real.

With basket in hand, Dad collected the girls and headed up to the house. Dad explained to Lois that he wanted to check this colored glass out to see if it was safe for the girls to play with. She agreed and thought it was a smart idea as well. With all that glass around, making sure it wasn't radioactive or polluted sounded like a good idea, Lois told Dad.

Mom and Grandma had loaded the girl's things into the motorhome they rented for the trip back, so after goodbyes, Mom, Dad, and the girls left to go home. Their drive was going to take two weeks to get home. They planned on sightseeing, and a day at Disney World, on their way back home. It also ended up giving Dad more time to look at the gems. On day 3 of their trip, the girls and their Mom were sleeping in the back of the motor home, when Dad decided to take a detour.

Dad knew of a park in Arkansas that offered "Search for your own diamonds!". It was called Diamond State Park, and they had special equipment that could check to see if the stones Dad had in his basket were real stones or commercial glass like Lois thought. The detour only took 8 hours which he drove at night while Mom and the girls slept.

In the morning after they had arrived at Diamond Stare Park, Dad explained to Mom what his suspicions were about the stones. They chose a couple of smaller stones of each color to test. On the off chance they were real stones, it would not be a good idea to test the larger stones and draw unwanted attention. Dad assumed that if the small stones were real, then the larger stones would be also because they all looked the same and were unusually heavy.

Dad's back story about the stones was that his father had been in lapidary, and these were in his estate when he passed. After all these years, Dad decided to see if they were real. It turned out to be a good thing they only brought in the smaller stones. The smaller stones they tested were indeed real. From what the gem tester said, the stones were some of the finest he had seen in years. They were all flawless and worth a fortune.

As it turned out every stone, and every color stone was real. They knew for sure the clear were diamonds, the green stones were emeralds, the red stones were ruby, and very possibly the blue stones were the rarest of all, blue diamonds, but would take additional testing to be sure. Dad had to leave the testing lab quickly, because a crowd was gathering, and the questions were mounting. Now that he knew the stones were real, Dad wanted as little attention as possible, since there were many more stones in the motorhome, and they were much bigger too. More stones, bigger stones, and hundreds more at Lois's cottage meant more money than Dad had ever imagined. Dad informed Mom that it was mandatory to head back to Lois's and inform her.

Mom, Dad, and the two girls pulled back into Lois's driveway 2 days later. Dad told Mom they were not going to stop at a pay phone to call Lois and let her know they were coming back, for fear someone might be listening in. Dad drove the 14 hours straight to Lois's with two stops for gas. He felt nervous with stones worth so much money in that RV with his kids and wife, so he kept going until they pulled into her driveway at 9 PM.

Mom went to the door and rang the bell. Lois took a couple of minutes to answer. Once she saw who it was, she immediately opened the door and asked what was wrong. Mom told her everything was fine, they decided to head back to her, so they could have an important conversation. Before Lois could ask what about, Dad came in with a little sleeping girl in each arm. Once the girls were sleeping in their beds, Dad asked Lois to sit.

"Oh, my, tell me you aren't having troubles, are you?" Asked Lois.

"Gosh no," said Dad. "This is bigger and more life-altering." He had a serious look on his face.

Dad proceeded to tell Lois that he had suspected the glass was actually not industrial glass, but natural gemstones. He told her how they went to a lab and had stones tested to see if they were real, or glass. They are not your regular gemstones, but flawless and worth a fortune. Dad went on to tell her that there were most likely hundreds of millions of dollars worth of gemstones in and around her cottage. And he almost begged her to please tell him where she got them.

Lois listened to Dad's story, then sat and thought for a minute, before saying, "It is late tonight, and I need the light to show you where I got the stones. Let us have breakfast in the morning, then I shall show you the secret."

By the time Dad got to the kitchen in the morning, everyone else but he was up, sitting at the table. Dad was exhausted from all the driving and all he wanted was coffee. Once he had his coffee, Dad sat, munched a cinnamon roll, and watched his girls play.

Lois suggested Dad finish his coffee before she told him a story. She said it would be better if he was fully awake before hearing what she had to say. Dad looked at her strangely then finished his coffee, quickly.

When Dad finished his coffee, he washed his cup, put it in the dish drain, then sat across from Lois, and said, "All right I'm ready," he paused "I think," he added.

Lois spent the next half an hour telling Mom and Dad everything. She told of the flowers first, then the trading of stones. Lois also asked the girls to verify her story. Of course, it took a bit of explaining to the girls, it was now ok for Mom and Dad to know everything about the Sasquatch. When they were done Lois asked everyone to follow her. Once she opened the hidden door the girls ran through. Mom and Dad followed slowly because if Lois and the girls were telling the truth, they were about to come face-to-face with Sasquatch.

The grotto was empty except for the girls. Lois went to the cottage and drove the piano out onto the deck. Once the piano was ready to play, Lois suggested the girls take Mom and Dad to a moss bed and wait. The girls both reminded their parents that the Sasquatch was friendly and not to scream when they saw them, because it might hurt the Sasquatchs' feelings. Lois smiled at that thought.

"I seriously can't believe I am actually sitting here waiting for Sasquatch to show up. If it wasn't for the stones being real, none of this would make sense," said Dad. "If this a joke Lois, it is the best joke ever."

As Lois started playing the piano, she told Mom and Dad she had asked the Sasquatch to avoid the grotto, so Mom and Dad wouldn't see them, which might mean it would take a bit longer than normal for them to come. Almost immediately after saying that the first adult female came into the grotto. Within 10 minutes there were 7 young Sasquatch and 10 adult females in the grotto. The girls ran up to the young ones right away, gave hugs all around, then held their hands while they led them to Mom and Dad.

Mom was speechless, and Dad kept muttering, "They are real," as the Sasquatch filed in. The laughing and skipping girls brought the small Sasquatch over to Mom and Dad. It turned out to be impossible for Mom not to accept the little Sasquatch that held its arms out for Mom to hold it. Mom melted as soon as the little thing clung tight and almost purred it was so happy. Dad stared like it was a dream, then he stood. Dad stood 6-foot-2 inches and every female there was at least a foot taller. The Sasquatch were quite gentle, but their size was imposing. Mom and Dad had been visiting for about 20 minutes, Dad was feeling relaxed when a loud noise arose in the jungle from the opposite side of the pool the cottage was on.

Lois smiled knowing what was coming and was certain that if anything was going to make Dad afraid, it was going to be the thing making the noise, that was coming their way. Both girls and the young Sasquatch realized what was coming and began chanting Gu, Gu, Gu, Gu is coming. Dad was standing next to a female sasquatch when Gu broke through the jungle wall. When all 10-foot-tall, 1200-pounds of pure muscle, came into view Dad ducked behind the female Sasquatch. Lois laughed at Dad, while the girls and young Sasquatch ran to Gu to greet him.

There was no way to prepare someone for their first meeting with Gu. There was no comparable animal. He was literally twice the size of a normal gorilla, two feet taller than a polar bear, and could pick up a car. But Gu is a gentle giant, as Mom and Dad were about to see as their little girls were right then reaching him. Gu knelt down and greeted his little troupe, including Mom and Dad's girls. They watched in amazement as this huge beast gently ruffled the heads of all the little ones, he even allowed the Sasquatch youth to climb his fur. The human girls weren't as strong as the Sasquatch kids, so Gu scooped each of them up in his gigantic hands. The girls looked like little dolls in his hands. Gu bent down and kissed each girl on the head, then each girl gave his huge face a hug and kisses. Once he set them down, they ran with the Sasquatch kids back to the moss beds for more music.

Dad and Mom stood and stared in amazement while Gu showed such sweet affection to their girls, but as he approached them, their fears rose a bit. Lois had not stopped playing the piano since they got there, but she did change the tunes. She purposely played scary music while Gu approached Mom and Dad, to make them more nervous. With Mom and Dad's backs to her, she stopped playing for a second to signal Gu and tell him to pick up Mom and Dad. When Gu figured out what her plan was, he smiled big.

Dad saw Gu's big grin and was trying to figure out if Gu was growling, or if he was going to be eaten, when with a swift move he was suddenly 10 feet in the air and staring at the biggest face he'd ever seen. The look on Mom and Dad's faces must have been the most terrified expression because Gu started laughing immediately. When Gu laughs, it is not a quiet affair. Gu's laughter can be heard for miles if he's not careful, and this was one of those times.

The girls and the other Sasquatch, as well as Lois, began laughing at the spectacle. Mom and Dad took a bit longer to find the humor in the situation though. Gu's laughter slowed and he set Mom and Dad back down. Once they were safely on the ground, Gu ruffled Mom's hair and rubbed Dad's bald head. When you looked at Gu's smile, you knew it was sincere and relaxed.

Lois introduced Gu to Mom and Dad, and explained, that he understood English, but had difficulty forming words, so he uses sign language. He uses a cross between the Sasquatch sign language and the human American Sign language. Dad held out his hand to Gu to show he was ok. Gu reached down and touched Dad's hand, in acknowledgment, then turned and left the grotto, and let out one more laugh as he disappeared.

"That was the most extraordinary event of my life," said Dad.

He picked me up as easily as I used to pick up our girls when they were babies. I am so looking forward to seeing him again."

The family had been in the grotto for a couple of hours by the time the Sasquatch left. Once all of them had disappeared back into the jungle, Lois suggested the family head back up for lunch, and talk about the future, now that her secret was out.

While they ate, Lois talked about the flowers being traded for apples, then the stones, and that the flowers were worth a fortune. She explained she had a deal where she delivered flowers and they deposited money, big money, into an offshore account, so it can't be traced. She wasn't worried about taxes, it was the rare flower buyers that would do anything to find where the flowers came from, so she had an account set up for her. The money was going to be used to take care of the Sasquatch. Now that the stones were real and worth a bigger fortune, there was more than enough to protect them.

Dad asked Lois if she could help him talk to Gu and see if he would tell us where they found the stones. Maybe if he understood the stones could be used to provide safety for his troupe, he would tell us. Lois thought that was a good idea and decided to ask the next time Gu showed up.

## 16

## DAD TRAVELS TO OTHER SASQUATCH VILLAGES

The next time Gu made his normal, but usual spectacular appearance, Lois signaled him to come sit for a talk. She also had one of the juvenile Sasquatch that could speak English well enough, she could help translate for Gu when he couldn't speak the word. Gu had not spent time in the reading and vocabulary sessions like the other Sasquatch, but he was a smart Sasquatch. He picked up English by listening to others talk, and by paying attention to the flashcards. He understood quite a lot but couldn't speak too easily, so Lois made a point of learning some of the sign language Gu used. Once Lois was able to get Gu to understand the pretty stones and flowers would help the Sasquatch to get food and safety from humans, he was more than willing to disclose the whereabouts.

Gu explained that the Sasquatch have been collecting the things humans throw away, lose, or bury, for as long as their stories tell. Sometimes, they find things on the beaches that wash ashore. There have been many boxes that float on the big water that break apart and drop the pretty things. Sometimes the humans bury little boxes with pretty rocks and heavy shiny metal things. Gu said, his kind has been collecting human things for as long as humans have been coming to their area and they have many caves where they keep the pretty human things they find.

When Gu finished, Dad looked at Lois, and asked, "Did he say boxes on big water and little boxes humans bury with pretty rocks and heavy shiny metal?"

"I am pretty sure he did," said Lois.

"I would be willing to bet, the boxes on the big water that break, are shipwrecks, and the little boxes they buried, are treasure chests that humans buried, and the Sasquatch dug up," Dad said.

"You have to be right," said Lois.

"Now I am curious about the many caves Gu is talking about," said Dad, "and I think I need to see if Gu will take me around to see them."

"I can only imagine the treasures they have found over the years," said Mom. "I'm not saying I want the first choice of the jewelry, but it would be nice to see and hold some real treasures," Mom gave a silly smile.

"I'm not going to lie, I'm with you Mom," said Lois, "I wouldn't mind having some fancy pirate treasure jewelry myself. I can imagine having a small jewelry box full of real queens' treasures on my bathroom counter," Lois added, while she pretended to be modeling fancy jewelry.

"If there are a lot of caves, and they have lots of treasure, then the Sasquatch have just made sure they can protect themselves," announced Mom. "If Gu will let us use some of their treasure to purchase land around here, then we can create a safe home for the Sasquatch.

Dad looked at Gu, and asked him "if it was possible for him to show where the caves are, and possibly bring back some of the lost human things they found, so they can make the Sasquatch safe from humans."

Gu thought for a moment, then said, "Yes, I will show you if you can make Sasquatch safe." "It will be many days of travel, and you will need your human things for the walk. It will take 10 days travel time to see all the caves." Gu added.

Dad spent a couple of days preparing for the trip with Gu. Dad needed clothes for 10 days, and a good amount of food, although Gu promised there would be plenty of food for Dad to eat along the way. Dad chose to be safe and bring enough energy bars to make sure he had enough.

Gu and Dad said goodbye to their families. Gu and Dad were going to travel alone. Gu said it was easier to keep an eye on just one human traveler. He also said he did not want to bring females because we were going to meet other males, and he didn't want any trouble with competition. He did say the other Sasquatch knew of humans, so Dad would be safe with him.

Gu walked silently most of the time as they traveled the railroad tracks. He said he was listening for any humans that might be nearby. Gu explained his group came from up north into Florida after the humans put in railroad tracks. He said the Sasquatch traveled the tracks because it was easier than walking through the thick jungle. The Sasquatches that were here are a smaller size than the ones in Gu's troupe. Most of the native Sasquatch were the size of humans, and thin, whereas Gu is more than twice the size of the biggest male native Sasquatch. He went on to say that he is the leader of all the Sasquatch within a 10-day walk.

On the morning of the second day, GU and Dad reached the first Sasquatch treasure cave. There were a dozen Sasquatch around the cave when they arrived. Gu told Dad that the Sasquatch there knew they were coming because an hour earlier he heard them announce their approach. Dad could never get used to the ability of the Sasquatch to hear and smell as good as a dog.

Gu stood 4 feet taller than the biggest native Sasquatch, and they were not much heavier than Dad. Dad didn't feel as intimidated around the new Sasquatch, because they were so similar to human size. Another difference with the native Sasquatch is their fur is not as thick or beautiful as Gu and his troupe. Dad assumed it was because the native Sasquatch lived in the dense jungle, and a smaller size made life easier for traveling. They were thinner as was their hair because of the heat. Smaller and thinner bodies dissipate heat better than larger bodies.

After the greetings, they entered the cave, which was larger than Dad had anticipated. He had anticipated the need for a flashlight, so he brought a solar rechargeable. He didn't want to worry about extra batteries, so this was the best choice.

There were moss beds in the cave as well as stacks of the things the Sasquatch have been collecting, which humans lost over the last 500 years in Florida. Gu had explained they often watched humans bury pretty things, then dug them up after the humans left. Sometimes they find shipwrecks and collect the things that wash ashore.

Dad and Gu inspected the treasures for an hour before Gu said it was time to leave or they wouldn't have time to see the other caves. Dad realized there was more treasure in that cave than would fit in a 20-foot moving van, and there was so much gold that a normal box truck wouldn't be able to carry it all. There were piles of gemstones of every color and size. Some were even already cut. The amount of incredible jewelry was beyond belief. There had to be hundreds of millions of dollars in treasure in just this one cave, which meant, the total sum for all caves must be uncalculable.

Over the next 9 days, Dad and Gu visited 20 such caves, like the first. Some of the caves were bigger and some were smaller, but all held hundreds of millions of dollars of gold, gems, pearls, and incredible jewelry. Dad was certain that some of the jewelry was from kings and queens, because it was fancy with huge gems, and there were even a few king and queen crowns.

Dad only brought a dozen bags of the fanciest king's jewelry, gems, pearls, and gold coins. Dad decided to bring a good sample of the gold coins that looked the rarest. Gu had a few of the native Sasquatch follow us back to Lois's home to the grotto, and they each carried bags of treasure. Gu loaded a wood wagon with bags and pulled it. When they arrived back at the grotto, everyone was excited to meet the native Sasquatch. The humans were glad they were so small, and Lois suggested they could wear human clothes, a hat, and maybe shave their face and they would look human from a distance. It's true if the native Sasquatch were shaved and in human clothes while walking around the community at night, they might be mistaken for a human if they were far enough away.

Dad, Gu, and the native Sasquatch laid out all the treasure they brought. The treasure covered an area that was 25 feet by 5 feet. Lois and the other senior humans who have been working with the sasquatch stood and stared at the treasure. The king's jewelry was too much of a temptation for some of the ladies, including Lois, and both granddaughters, and they all began modeling the fancies, like little girls playing dress up. More than one person asked if they could keep what they were wearing. Gu and Dad laughed and said at the same time, that there were enough jewels, everyone there could have a suitcase full.

Lois looked at Dad and asked, "Was there really that much?"

"Let me put it this way," Dad started. "there is so much treasure in those caves, that everyone here could bring a suitcase home and barely put a dent in the treasure." "Honestly, we could and should make sure all our friends here that help with the Sasquatch, get a share so that they do not have any financial needs," Dad added.

Lois's granddaughters heard Dad say that and decided they each needed princess's crowns and began searching for the treasures. The seniors standing around looked at Dad with questioning looks, so Dad assured them, that once they sold some of these things, they would make sure everyone involved would get the financial help they needed or wanted. Dad wanted the seniors to be honest if they needed financial help because there was going to be enough to spare.

Dad told everyone they needed to be cautious about how they sell the things, so no one finds out where they came from. The last thing they needed was a bunch of people snooping around, trying to learn where the treasures came from. They also didn't want to flood the market. Dad would get a group together and catalog the treasure, then determine how best to sell it, to raise money for the Sasquatch.

By the time Dad had finished explaining the plan, the girls and 6 Sasquatch kids, were all covered in fancy jewelry. The humans and Sasquatch were all laughing at the kids, because all of the kids had so much jewelry on, they could barely stand or walk. Lois's youngest granddaughter was lying flat on her back and couldn't sit up. She had put so much on that she fell backward and couldn't sit back up without removing a few pounds of heavy gold jewelry.

Lois looked at the spectacle, "Looks like we have our jewelry models for when we want to sell the stuff."

The next day, Lois sent out a flyer to all the people who lived in the Bear Creek community, asking if anyone living there had experience in rare coins, precious stones, and antique jewelry. Lois felt it was smarter to find experts in their community rather than bringing people in from the outside. After a week, Lois had received responses from 7 people who had experience in those areas.

Over the next few months, Lois watched the experts set up and sell these special treasures. What they had done was contact their friends, and had them contact the buyers, so that no one had a connection with anything at Bear Creek. They set up many complex offshore accounts so that even the government wouldn't be able to trace the source.

At the six-month mark, the head accountant told Lois that the 25 offshore accounts had a total of $200 million apiece deposited, and he didn't know if they could hide any more money. He suggested that they invest, or buy property, to spread the money out and decrease the chance of getting caught. After their conversation, Lois had an idea.

The Bear Creek golf course was not being used much, because there weren't many seniors that played at this time, which gave Lois an idea. She was going to buy the golf course and that land would give the Sasquatch a massive land buffer to protect them from human incursion. Lois instructed the accountant to start a non-profit company to buy the golf course and close it as an environmental statement. They will make a press announcement stating they bought the golf course, and let it return to its natural state after they demolish the clubhouse.

To say that a few golfers were upset would be a big understatement. Lois had the accountant give each of the golfers enough money to join the really expensive and fancy golf club a few miles away. Since the fancy course was much better, and they got free memberships, the golfers were happy with the deal. She had the accountant include a new golf cart that was kept at the golf course.

Since they had sold all the treasures from Dad and Gu's first trip to the caves, Lois suggested Dad and Gu take another walk to the nearest caves and restock. Dad suggested they bring along a few of the experts, so they can help pick and choose the best to bring. Lois asked Gu if it was possible, for he and a few other Sasquatch could lead the trek to the caves and help the senior experts that would be going along. Many of the senior experts were mid-70 years old and a long hike would not be possible. Gu assured her that they would use their wagons to help get the seniors to the caves safely.

Gu, Dad, 6 other Sasquatch, who would help carry and pull the wagons, as well as 4 of the Bear Creek residents who were experts in Gemstones, rare coins, and jewelry left two days later. The trip lasted a week, and everyone on the trek had a wonderful time. The senior humans said it was the most exciting time they had ever experienced. They told of meeting hundreds of Sasquatch and seeing the most spectacular scenery in Florida. Each cave was one surprise after another.

One cave sent an expert into a laughing fit because it was so fabulous. The cave was filled with extremely old weapons, that must have been from a pirate shipwreck. There was mint condition, blunder busts, hand muskets, swords, and even a couple of wooden legs. Around the outer area of the cave, the Sasquatch had used old wooden furniture from ships, to make the cave livable, even for a human.

Most of the caves were within a couple hundred feet of spring-fed pools, so the Sasquatch could stay near the cave to protect their treasures. Once Gu explained the humans were using their found things to protect the Sasquatch, they all agreed to share with the humans.

When the traveling treasure hunters returned, all the wagons were carrying their maximum load, and even the Sasquatch was strained a bit pulling the loads. That is except Gu, who was literally twice the size of any other Sasquatch on the trip, and 4 times as strong. It wasn't unusual to see Gu pulling a wagon with each arm, to give the smaller Sasquatch a rest.

When the final tally of the treasure was totaled, the amount was staggering, and almost enough to buy the whole state of Florida. The accountants set up dozens of shell companies, to hide the money. They even bought Bear Creek from the owners, so they could have total control of the community, without interference, from outside the community.

Starting after Dad returned from his first trip with Gu, checking out the Sasquatch treasure caves, they began buying all the land around the Bear Creek senior community. By 2023 Lois and her group owned more land than any other property owner in Florida, which gave a massive safe area for the Sasquatch. One piece of land they bought for the Sasquatch's new preserve was the neighborhood golf course. Lois never liked golf anyway and thought their land should be used for parks for the public to use, not chasing a little white ball.

The park manager stayed on with her husband as residents after they retired. For the most part, it was easy keeping the existence of the Sasquatch secret, because no one in the community wanted to lose their wonderful Sasquatch friends.

# 17

## SASQUATCH FOREVER SAFE PLACE

Over the years as technology advanced, the Bear Creek community added surveillance equipment all over the Sasquatch preserve. It turned out the best deterrent to keep humans away was dense jungle. If a human was detected coming into the Sasquatch area, the most effective way to drive them out and make sure they never returned, was to have the Sasquatch scare them. It was rare that a Sasquatch needed to be seen to scare them. They threw rocks, and logs, and would let loose with an incredibly loud Sasquatch scream. Gu's scream could be heard for over a mile, but even the smaller ones could fill the dense jungle with sounds that made the humans flee in panic. They flee so fast sometimes, that they leave their personal things, which the Sasquatch collects and stores in a cave for future use.

In 2023 Lois reached 94 years of age and decided to turn over all control to the younger group, including her granddaughters. The younger group has known the Sasquatch for almost 40 years, and they felt the Sasquatch were their family.

The latest plan the granddaughters and the group that leads the community are debating the merits of changing the name of Bear Creek to Sasquatch Heaven. Lois and the older seniors laughed, saw the potential problems that could come up, and sat back to see what was going to happen next.

# ABOUT THE AUTHOR

Patrick Talmadge Sr. has always been a late bloomer. His growth didn't cease until he was over 21 years old. He reached his pinnacle as a national and world-class masters middle-distance runner at the age of 37, when he won his first master's national track and field championship in the 800-meter run.

At 47, Patrick earned his Bachelor of Arts degree and made history as the oldest NCAA cross-country runner. Seven years later, at 54, he returned to college to pursue a Master's degree in Psychology. During this time, he ran the mile in track, once again setting a record as the oldest NCAA track and field runner. He received his Master's degree in Psychology at 57. At the age of 66, he embarked on his writing journey.

Patrick taught himself to read at the tender age of three and a half and has been an avid reader ever since. With a keen interest in all fields of science, science fiction, and fantasy, he amassed a wealth of knowledge that would later prove invaluable when he began writing. Throughout his 20s and 30s, Patrick devoured two to three books a day. Upon graduating from graduate school in 2011, he retired from competitive running and felt a growing desire to write the stories that had been simmering within him.

In November 2021, spurred on by the love of his life, Patrick began his writing career. By July 2023, he had completed an adult four-book science fiction series about Sasquatch, a four-book children's series on the same subject, and a standalone novel about a senior community that befriends a troupe of Sasquatch.

Patrick possesses a unique ability to write multiple stories simultaneously, allowing him to modify and adjust interconnected narratives for clarity when writing a series. With a bit of luck, Patrick will continue to pursue his passion for writing for the rest of his life, or at least until his computer gives out.

# ALSO BY PATRICK TALMADGE

### Hidden Mountain Chronicles

*Sasquatch Race*

*Sasquatch Prison Diary*

*Tenino Caverns*

*Sasquatch Home Planet*

### Sasquatch Chronicles

*Hunter and Noah vs. Sasquatch Vol. 1*

*Hunter and Noah vs. Sasquatch Vol. 2*

*Hunter and Noah vs. Sasquatch Vol. 3*

*Hunter and Noah vs. Sasquatch Vol. 4*

### Sasquatch Senior Community Series

*Sasquatch Senior Community*

*Sasquatch Senior Community: Lois and Mel the Beginning*

*Sasquatch Senior Community: The Early Years*

*Sasquatch Senior Community: The Middle Years*

# AFTERWORD

Go to hangaripublishing.com to learn more about the Authors and stay up to date with their newest releases.

www.ingramcontent.com/pod-product-compliance
Lightning Source LLC
Chambersburg PA
CBHW071215120626
46546CB00006B/2568